Bridge Pamphlet
No. 6

The Hungry
Ghost Festival

Jen Campbell is from a village just outside Newcastle upon Tyne. She graduated from Edinburgh University with an MA in English Literature in 2009 and now lives in North London. She works in an antiquarian bookshop and her book *Weird Things Customers Say In Bookshops* was published in April 2012 by Constable and Robinson.

The Hungry Ghost Festival [a traditional Chinese festival]. On the 15th night of the seventh lunar month, the boundaries between the living and the dead break down, and the dead visit the earth looking for food and entertainment.

Jen Campbell's festival celebrates the presence of the past, in this case childhood and adolescence in the North East, as it floats through the present adult consciousness.

The Hungry
Ghost Festival

JEN CAMPBELL

THERIALTO

ACKNOWLEDGEMENTS

Many thanks to the editors of the following, where several of these poems first appeared, *Agenda, The Delinquent, Ink Sweat and Tears, The Interpreter's House, Obsessed With Pipework, Poetry London, The Rialto*.

BRIDGE PAMPHLETS

This is the sixth in a series of *The Rialto* pamphlets designed to cross the gap between magazine and book publication for new writers or, for established writers, that between collections.

First published in 2012. Reprinted 2016.
The Rialto
PO Box 309 Aylsham Norwich
England NR11 6LN

ISBN 9780955127397

The Publisher acknowledges financial assistance from Grants For Arts.

LOTTERY FUNDED

The Rialto is a Registered Charity No. 297553
Typeset in Berling 10 on 12.5pt
Design by Starfish, Norwich
Printed by Micropress Limited, Halesworth, Suffolk
Cover illustration by Laura Barnard

For Mr Binz, who taught me haiku when I was nine

CONTENTS

KITCHEN

What would you do if I died right now, here, you asked,
your hand still resting on my thigh. Your eyes focused on the ceiling,
on the splash of curry sauce to the left of the light which doesn't work.
We could have been in a field.
A wooden spoon dug into my back.
I thought it funny.
Let's not talk of death where food is prepared, I said.

You turned away, stood up and opened the fridge.
The light shone past you. An outline of you

your feet tapping on the floor. Your mother would be home soon.
To her yellow and white check tea towels and her hand-painted bread bin

and her naked daughter standing like Jesus in front of the
refrigerator. I grabbed your foot.
Come on, your nipples'll freeze and you'll be cryogenically frozen.
There was a laugh somewhere, under your hair, as you toppled backwards
onto the floor and cupped my face.
So if I died, right here, now, you said – you'd freeze me?
Your eyes were grey, round. You were swimming and
I didn't know what you wanted me to do.

I'd keep you, I said. I'd keep you, right here.
Dead? You grinned. Where food is prepared?
Well then I'd eat you, I said, and you stared so deep I drowned
in a kitchen that wasn't there: I'd swallow down all the evidence of you.
I grabbed your hand.
We heard a key turn in a front door, somewhere by the shore.
I'd like that, you said, and then kissed me.

MEMORIES OF YOUR SISTER IN A FULL BODY WET SUIT

Letters had been found in bags. Cut and stick newspaper notes
like it's the movies. So we took her away.
She looked out of place against the motor. It was its corners,
and her hair as she pushed the back seats down flat to sit. Like a tank.
Before then, when I'd seen her, she'd just been showered.
I'd caught her eyes in vases, in newly-washed milk bottles
before you'd thrown them on the front step.
She used to dodge under tables. She preferred the ground.

We three sang along the road, an old fur coat across my knees.
All she wanted was to cradle old cassette covers. They opened
up with sound. Like a rolled up flannel you threw in water
'til it bloomed. My aunt bought those in bulk from the Disney store in town.
That was the nineties. Petals shoved into pores.
We'd scrub down in a shared bath until all the sins were drowned.
Amen. You sped up then to make sure all the cruel things got left behind.

The sea was far; you could guess it by the gulls. I spy on the run.
You took us to a lighthouse, her nose high in the air ten miles
before we pulled up. Her hands against the windows, making waves.
She never used to talk much. You said you always used to come here
before your mum found amber bottles on a top shelf.
Before the operation where your sister's legs were split - because she'd arrived
in this world swimming. Your dad looking for a receipt.

Now the kids call her selkie until they make it stick.
Her left leg is weaker, only half the bones. Henry said
she must've done a bad thing, back when. Like you can bottle karma
and shower in it. So we left a canoe strapped to the car roof.
Enough cat food out so it'd be there when we made it back.
Your mother would be sleeping. No more bad luck. No more dead fish.

Our bags were full of lycra. You blew bubbles, and she grinned,
your knuckles red. We changed our clothes right in the car park
with all its people watching, their eyes tracking scars
that snaked all up her legs and down again as scissors.

You grabbed the camera. We put our faces through those portrait boards
a sailor and a mermaid.

She jumped into the sea as though parting water
and it listened. You took my hand, said you'd forgotten soap.
I remembered arm bands like blood pressure monitors,
the pounding in my ears. Water shooting up my nose and the taste of anaesthetic.

THE MOUNTAIN MINERS

We ran up the hill
to prove the rumours were true.

I found the seagull splayed out,
stomach reaching for the sun.

We'd been told that if you touched its neck
you'd never get diseases. We could spy

the sea from there - the topless windmill
that locked up ten of Emily's screams.

Tommy was the first to touch it: its gullet
stinking of the fish gulped down

at the bucket docks of the Tyne.
I once saw a rat there as big as my fist. We recoiled

and searched his knuckles for maggots.
There weren't any. But that wouldn't make me kiss him.

CROSS-HATCH

It was said a girl I sat beside in biology
charged for sex on Cleadon Hills.

You could see the heads of those from my folks'
top room. We'd peek out from there to see

if boys would walk right past the pond and along
up by the special school. We did not spy it, our noses

burning as we rested them on top of the radiator.
We were birds perching. When it rained I wondered

if she took a tent and if she hitched her skirt up. The thing is
she never came to Guides. Lizzy told me of oral sex on the 525 home

and lit the Bunsen burners up in class. We always wanted
to ask if she went up there for fun. If it was true

the topless windmill was lived in. If she had chiselled
her name on the half-eaten oak bench, and if the grass was long.

She'd walk the corridors, a price tag on her head. Our mouths
were black holes then. Tongues moved quickly throughout our school.

THE ANGEL

was moulded when I was seven, further down the country.
It was the same day we copied the world in Lego.
She was made in parts, then glued together
hauled back up again on the back of a truck, sleeping.
We mocked her on the way home from Thurston Outdoor Education Centre
flapping our arms like wings as the mini-bus rocked.
She is rusted like ridges along the tops of tin cans.
Ten thousand naked tin cans.
Birds try to bring her hair so they can make homes in the ears she does not have.
Her arms reach out to touch the sky. I think she does not touch it.

BIRDHOUSE

One of those Sunday afternoons no one knows how to use. Picking rosemary
in oversized wellingtons. Green ones. *Grease* and *Singing in the Rain* parading
out. Mam and dad arguing over lamb about which to glue their daughters to.
The carving knife lying by my sister's bear. I peer through rain drops on the
living room window. Warp a birdhouse I won. I'd painted leaves colours of
refracted light. Given cloud edges. Beetroot dipped. A photographer'd come
to picture it and me. For the Echo, both of us. A chipped fag half-hanging out
his mouth. He never took it out. Knelt on the patio paving with ten clicks and
cracks. *'Smile, pet.'* A red blue yellow waistcoat knitted by grandma. Non-flying
ladybirds as buttons. I coaxed my bird lips upwards, then the flash. Eight years
of scraped knees. We put Grease on at school. Danny played by the campest
lad and we couldn't sing the big songs 'cause of money. During scenes the car
doors slammed. Pony tail competitions backstage in lycra catsuits. Fruit gums
for those who got it highest. Just grocers' cardboard between teenage girls
ripping off their clothes, the boys on the left. Cathy spied my dad nipping out
for a cigarette. Used to swear he never smoked. Didn't take an umbrella and
somewhere it was prom night. It was hot out there in the auditorium. It was
raining outside.

ANGEL METAL

We stand underneath and pray to her.
We do not know why we pray. Sometimes
the sheep come to look before the fires start.
It is hard, the grass. It's the frost here.
We are all of us the worm on a higher ground.
You hold my hand like it's the theatre.
The applause is too low down
winding under us like electric rabbits. You
pick my arms up and spread them out
so we are matching. Our woollen scarves
touch our noses - catch our breath
like cloth balloons. We dig our feet into the soil
and stamp down into the very deep.
Somewhere below, the river sleeps with a lady
screeching. She has arms that could carry boulders
to the edge of cliffs. We wait for her
to throw us down. Our parents, stiff, pretend
they are not watching. They sit on sofas behind
their damning newspapers. We are not children.
We wait alone in the coldest times while people read.
They say we have taken something
they can never put back inside of us. They say
we are building blocks, and purse their ragged lips.
I picture barren fields transformed into supermarkets
with bars across their naked windows.
I am warm inside. We wait.
We fill our pockets up with frozen peaches.

WRITTEN IN MY 1999 DIARY: NEWCASTLE FUTURES

We lost our childhood, up on the
        hilltops   rebuilt
      a blinking river eye
across The Baltic, watching out
      for the Chase club.
Matthew jumped there, lost his shoes
         his body
      and him supplied a week long paparazzi shot.
         Then chippy wraps.
And at our comp. the head boy sprouting
        ADAM from pockets that his mother
           stitched.
      Like he's the first man.
The school clinging on to cliff tops out
        the North sea. Wind farms
of hands which turn but don't make bread.
      Fists are kneading on the bus
           home.
Shouts of faggot. Jackets piling in the aisle
      like rotting veg.
      They all roll, shout out their fathers'
        favourite words.

WHEN WE FOUND THE TIDE

We carried red buckets across the power-washed paving stones
even though your brother said we shouldn't
bail out the salt water grains
when the garden was joined with the sea, hinged on soil,
and it had been raining

like the times when we, my sister and I, sat in that basket
with the dirty clothes, between Blue Peter and dinner,
with an umbrella
spotting shells on blue carpet in my mother's turquoise blouse.
Like that bird and that cat in that mini streamliner
and we were both then queens of the whole wide world.

But that gap between a show and some food is now twenty two years
of painted toe nails going hungry and, when I met you,
I was wearing Converse. It was such a waste of glitter
but you didn't care, and it's probably best because you stood

all over my shoes by mistake, took me out for chips and told
me you owned the pier at Brighton. That lights were your thing
some crap line about turning things on,
about flipping my switch, but all I could really see was
that bit of ketchup on your lip. The acidic smell of vinegar.

We fill buckets with water we made overflow, taking photos
on our phones as we tip
and try to make salt water castles
and you tell me you own all the water in the world
and that you are prepared to share it.

That this water is the sea and the lawn our pea-green boat
that you'd upgraded to first-class just for me.
And then we run to the house
where our shoes are waiting, blades of grass standing
right between our feet.

GAMBIT

I don't remember talk of finger nail clippings
clinging to the sofa patterns. Of your face crowning
through the door,

red queen snapping: could I shove my limbs
behind the cushions
with the one penny pieces and June's mini-milk sticks,

where you'd put half an hour in with
loose change for moments like these - when your high
heels are on backwards, a taxi on the meter and

you're trying not to mention
that red wine stain. I've got it covered

with my sock, a furniture tombola, with your hair up in rollers
and you will be late, trailing breadcrumbs, but you kiss me:

check mate, and I check, all thumbs hitched
on a chewing gum wrapper
rummaging around for some borrowed time.

POLYPHEMUS

Our eyes learn to play the harmonica
whilst our mouths hang
      the gentle hum of those   who swim in jars
         stare upwards   orbit rooms.

The glass-maker did not praise this
taxidermy of human skin. The video
      speaks the mutants, dead   the tailed-girl
         they are here   for you (but they are not you)

The calf's nose is stripped as leather
to stare out with its one eye.
          A hunting trophy
        our baited fingers   we hang off them
        pedal stale air   its breath on glass.

LIKE A FISH OUT

I have pictures of us kissing tv screens. June spent trying to map the weight in your eyes. Where it ran to: those etch-a-sketches. Shook you up in black and white. Beds in separate rooms for you to lie down in when your mum called. We stop-watched those. Spent our lunch times in catsuits. Your skin scaling: peeling. All the water drained; staring out of a classroom window at the water. Some days, I remember, we'd go over to the cliff tops. Just to look and to feel. The sun light-bulbing on a netball pitch. Some days I look at you. Your mother and her pity-me-face next to a microwave nodding to the seconds before the ping. She brings soup to your room so you're not dehydrated. So you have no need to look out the window at the water. So you have no need. No need at all.

LILY ROSE

She hangs up still behind
them. The sky is her face. Blinded
by last week's sunlight trapped
in the living room curtains. The
air is close now. It cuts around her
fallen smile in the way her father
would caress. She is less now. More
so. More or less, with one foxglove
mitten reaching out for the light
switch. They come now, the neighbours
and all who once wished they could sail
in the billows of her off-white frock.
They do not bring one prayer book.
They peer through the yellow spatted
curtains. The lace. The larger ones gasp
to hide the giggles. A pop of apple
bubblegum and their misplaced glee. Have you heard?
Can you see! Someone orders Chinese
from down Holloway Road and they gather on
the floor, gaping upwards. Eat it in.
Some talk with their mouths full.
Food spirits litter the air. Her patent leather shoes
and shining buckles brace themselves.
The closest ones tap the glass between them and her.
Palm it. She turns on the spot. Cut out
from a jewellery box. They ooh and ahh, hold a metre
ruler up to the glass against rotating thighs.
It is five days before the police are called. When asked
what the fuss is, the watchers say:
she is a fish now, kick, kick, kicking. We cannot save her.

SPRINGTIME CATCH

Up here, we're fierce friends with the sea.
If it calls our name
we let it hollow us out. At sunset
near the jetty you can spot
the teenagers by their thrown
clothes. Their sandpaper skin
half buried in the wind. The girls
on their backs. The still tide out.
Used wrappers like lollipop covers
and the car parks filled to the hilt
with rusty old trucks
borrowed from middle-aged fathers.
The boys and their limpet hair.

The seagulls line the pier and wait
for the pink bodies to mould
as angler fish. For their denim
to shed itself like dustbin
lids over rock pools.
For the young, clueless, blinking.
Those on the sand think of swimming
lessons at school. Holding
their noses and jumping like starfish.
Splashing their feet through the initial pool
that once had floating lemons.

They could hang from trees
and dive down from them.
Land on their stomachs to
have the wind punched out. Between
us - those watching from decks
of upside-down houses
and those filming behind the dunes -
we see who's the first to notice
they can't breathe underwater.

TREADING WATER

I was birthed in the Tyne on a fluorescent buoy
kept afloat by its placenta. Both of us ballooned.

My eye a coin of seagulls, mothering.

We all come out of these wombs
swimming: for six months we can breathe like that.

On his lunch my father threw crumbs from the Biscuit Factory.
A prayer I'd stay afloat. To begin with there were warm cookies.

Those first Sundays people with cameras came. Snapped me
screaming on my back. Like an apple bobbing before the pie.

I lay as a longboat twisting to reach our old Valhalla -
my plastic mother drowned below. The first word was anemone.

I farmed myself: a kick for every Christmas day
I wouldn't sit under a moulting tree. Some tried to baptise me

from the river banks, and The Baltic where locals looked out
from sky-top floors. Binoculars to count the salt I cupped.

Umbilically I was a long line of fishermen and lasses.
A northern starfish. A pink, fleshed bomb waiting for my tail to grow.

I smiled gums for ships I'd one day sink.
I hovered in the river mouth, touching neither one side nor the other.

THE ART OF SAVING OTHER PEOPLE

We never meant for her to give
birth inside a church. Pass the towels
you said, like you'd done this before.
The energy-saving light bulbs bouncing
off your hair gel.
We haven't got no towels, I said
looking round and seeing only paper stacks.
I considered swallowing them whole
to start a fire within myself.
Where are the people? you asked – abandoned
fishing rods by the holy font.
The three of us kneeling down on top
of knitted prayer mats.
We fed her ice cream to remind us of childhood days.
Between the yells and shooting pains
I counted candles. Twelve - half expecting
wings to come. For a bird to be birthed
out on the cold stone floor.
To have to take her home to mother inside a cage.
For her to whistle.
For the blue glass lambs to carol-sing.
In the car, before, we'd guessed some names
by traffic lights - bemused that we
could walk upright compared to animals.
Our breath is dragon smoke.
You could be a window, right now,
you said. Up there, high, in three bright colours.
Which colours? I said
seeing all of them in bloody orbs.
My hands, and yours, crushed chestnuts, roasting.
Her stomach an ark-sized orange fruit.

ULLAMBANA
[the hungry ghost festival]

for Poppa

When we sat on the hills that looked over my house
we saw Chinese lanterns we had not set free. They had
no name on their sides, just orange. They were a peaceful army.
These lanterns hold the name of a copper for the way they carry
themselves. Two metals hinged at the sides - a hip joint.
Like the Japanese flower *physalis alkekengi* hangs upside down
and patiently waits there.

Your hands used to move like rice paper.
'It must be jelly 'cause jam don't shake like that.'
You went to China and brought me dolls dressed up as air hostesses.
I have Yashica photos of you building nuclear plants, a pipe half in your mouth
and Wellington boots that covered the base of your suit.

For you, I signed a form to place my brain in a jar when I'm
done with it. They will lift it from my skull and see you.

If we were home now, I'd be looking out my bedroom window.
When I was three an owl hit the glass there and you can still
trace the outline of its feathers. I did not see it fall.
The lantern was postbox red then. It was a letter. At school we did an assembly
about the little match girl, and the next year I played a gangster.
You didn't mind which I was as long as there was music.

Over dinner my sister said to me 'When did dragons become extinct?'
and somewhere you were laughing. The lamp rose as a dragon tongue.
If I were in London I would not see this
but would light a candle. It's been a year, almost,
as the crow flies. This year it is the year of the rabbit.
I go and sit myself at the piano. Play Honky Tonk parade.

LOBSTER GIRL

i)
When we think, we think of beginnings

when I was a bairn and my folks took me to the circus:
showed me the clowns; their red faces,
bought me blue candy floss that melted all over my hands.

These hands could fly, their bandages unravelling.
I could be a bird, I said; I had the hooked nose for it,
shot out of the canon.
Boom baby.

It was only later I discovered I was born out of the sea.

ii)
In the beginning me and the world stood either side of telescopic geography – with
suns and moons, as frisbee jets caught under foot. We had to pass each other without
dropping time, salute across our running field. The embryonic path. The genetic pool.
The dawn and dusk of fingers crossing

iii)
and my fingers were trees.

That's how I think. Of branches
stuck together. Of joints shaped like elephants

which I felt-tipped faces on.
Where a hand is a tortoise: my palm its shell.

(It is strange to have something and not know how to name it
like a guest plonked in your kitchen for twenty four years.)

When the internet was born - a virus on wheels – I found it.
Its name fell out. You could Google the freak shows:

the staring faces of a family who held their hands up like meat.

In America: The Lobster Boy
who sat behind bars and the whole world watched.
Popcorn falling on weekend trips. A whole lot of weak knees.

Yet we stand now, as trees, as birds.
As land-walking sea-women. And
we are not caged. We fly.

WHAT HAPPENS WHEN I GO HOME

My mam said she'd seen you along the 35 route, the one that goes to Shields.
Neither of you were on the bus. That's beside the point.
She was busy hoisting brussel sprouts, tucked in those blue hair nets they come in
like they just fished them out the Wear. My brother said they probably do,
trying his best to ignore the Christmas music.

It's been a fair few years.
The council's gone all out this winter to cheer us up. Gathering all the jobs
and crying 'let there be light!' and, hey, all the closed down shops are lit
up like Christmas trees. H'way, eh?
We ooo and ahh on the pavement with our plastic bags, Christmas shopping,
take a slice of the Lambton Worm at the outside café, sizzling its way
between two pieces of doorstop bread. Chomp on down.
"We could take the boarded up signs for firewood." A snort-giggle,
chip fat dripping over the pavement, like we're eating eachothers' flesh.

It's just, we don't realise we're cooked already 'cause our skin's still violet,
the air humming blue with all the negative numbers.

By this time my mam'd reached the middle of the bridge
in full view of the football stadium where I used to spend my Saturdays.
And then she saw you, on the other side. She said you were wearing a dog-eared hat,
pushing yourself along as though racing the traffic.
Fingerless gloves gripping the wheels.
She would have said hello if it weren't for all the cars.
"I'll never forget what that woman did to that girl," she said,
on the phone, shoving the turkey into the freezer. Deader than dead,
the ping of her wedding ring on the edge of a bird's bone.
I felt sick. "When's your train?"

And I get all that 'well, you're in London now, aren't ya?' This Northern
hostility that isn't even reciprocated. Just like being an English student
in Edinburgh, and I'm over it.
"It's all the same," I fib, twirling the phone line round my broken finger.
But, here, the 35 goes to Clapham and I've never seen you there.

THE PATRON SAINTS OF ANIMALS

No one mentions the dead bird hanging in the hall.
Tommy takes a stick to it. Feathers fall across the rug
which our grandpa dragged over from the orchard fields.
Makes it smell of blood apples. Of carol-singing cheeks,
their glow nicked straight out of the freezer. We practice singing
in the basement, cool our hands on mother's solid stock.
In the kitchen, knives are sharpened up for beef joint,
chicken eggs in pots sit humming on the window ledge.

My task is putting prayers out on the napkins, like
a specials board. I divide the words up as I would cut grain.
No one crows for us in the morning, now. It is our job to always
wake ourselves. Mother calls this time our crystal dawn. It means
she often misses breakfast.
She feeds the kid goats at the table, out of bottles. Old body parts
we no longer need. Father reddens but does not speak of it.
Upstairs the top sow has the larger bath.

Tommy chimes out that it's one o'clock. He's found
Christmas crackers to break open on the hour. He puts
the plastic toys up on the mantelpiece. They sit between our cloven hooves.
Father brings our biggest cow in from the outside cold.
She clatters on the table top, breaking soup bowls under her.
I pinch my thigh and don't say a thing. Use a butter knife to file my dirty nails.
Father raises his prayer crown high. I remember days when those were pirate hats
and sometimes boats. We close our eyes and think
of animals, low bleatings sounding in our throats
like paper wrappers. Tommy's laughing at the joke he found.

Mother puts her palms out on the cow's warm flank, counts upwards
guessing meals. I think how many of us could fit inside and
be reborn with leather shoes.
There is a flutter in the hallway, grandpa's cough.
We could feed here for a long while, I think, then hang her udders up
on the chandelier. Fill them high with marzipan, and dance below.
We'd be barefoot on the broken plates, singing winter songs for food.